Legal Shorts. . . Not Briefs

Lawful Laughs from School and Practice

Luther Beauchamp
Illustrated by Joe McKeever

Kidiot Productions

Published by

Kidiot Productions
P. O. Box 10
Chiefland, Florida 32644
(352) 493-2525

DEDICATION

Dedicated to the memory of my brother,
W.O. Beauchamp, Jr.
who died July 19, 2000

W.O. was three years older but many years wiser. He served the last seven years of his life as circuit judge, the only resident of our county to have served as a circuit judge in modern times. Prior to that he had been the Levy County Court Judge from 1973-1993. He was "a firm but fair" judge.

When we were boys and after we became men my brother was a very worthy example and a positive influence for me and for others. His faithfulness as husband and father was never questioned.

W.O. closely followed the Biblical admonition of Micah 6:8:

> *"...to do justice, to love kindness, and to walk humbly with your God."*

Acknowledgments

Much of my inspiration for this book came from my fellow law students and my professors at Vanderbilt University; my law partners and my clients; as mentioned in the book, family friend and former Florida Attorney General Earl Faircloth; and my dear brother, W.O. Beauchamp, Jr., to whose memory this work has been dedicated.

Even with all of that inspiration, however, this book could not have been written without the help of my wife, Vera. As I tell my audiences when making my humor presentations, we have celebrated 68 years of marriage. That's 34 for her and 34 for me. A member of one audience responded, "I'll bet hers have been longer." That's probably right.

Thank you Vera, for your typing, your arranging, your editing and for your encouragement.

Thanks also to Joe McKeever for his great illustrations.

Contents

Preface

The study and practice of law are not usually thought to be laughing matters. Humor is often found in the eyes and ears of the beholder.

Behold! I have found much to laugh about during my preparation for and the practice of the legal profession. Really never having gotten the hang of it, after 32 years I'm still practicing.

This book preserves some of my favorite incidents related to my legal career. As you enjoy some of my funny experiences be reminded of your own. Whether you are a barrister, butcher, banker, barber or beggar, you have your stories that could bring smiles to others and to yourself as they are retold.

Some names have been changed to protect me from claims of libel and others just for the fun of it.

If this book brings happiness to only one person, that's not very many. My prediction is that it will be enjoyed by at least a dozen.

If you like this book tell a lot of people. If you don't like it, please keep quiet about it. You could hurt my chances of selling more books. That would be bad. I need the closet space.

PROFESSIONAL INFLUENCES

Why would anyone want to be a lawyer? While I cannot answer that question for anyone else, I believe I know some of the reasons I wanted to become a lawyer.

My father was a great fan of Perry Mason and always enjoyed trying to solve mysteries before they were dramatically revealed in the courtroom. Becoming another Perry Mason was never my specific objective but that program and my father's enthusiasm for the judicial process probably had an influence upon me and my brother, W. O., who later served as a circuit judge.

Another strong influence was a family friend, Earl Faircloth. "Mr. Earl," as my brother and I always called him, was born and reared in the Chiefland area. He rode the school bus Daddy drove even though he was only a few years younger than my father.

After graduating from Chiefland High School, Mr. Earl attended the University of Florida serving as President of the student body while earning his law degree. He settled in Miami to practice law and a number of years later was elected to the Florida House of Representatives. When not in legislative session, Mr. Earl continued his law practice.

When Faircloth had legal matters in our area he often would spend one or more nights in our home. My brother, W. O., and I admired him very much and enjoyed hearing the legal "war stories" he told.

Earl Faircloth had a significant influence on our vocational choices. We wanted to be a part of the profession we believed Mr. Earl represented very well.

W. O. worked one summer in Mr. Earl's Miami law office while he was in law school. I was given the privilege of working in the office of Attorney General Faircloth for a few months between my college graduation and my entry into Vanderbilt University School of Law.

LYING WHEN?

During a murder trial in Levy County, Mr. Earl was questioning the state's key witness against his client. After the witness answered, Faircloth pointed out that his answer that day was exactly opposite his answer to the same question presented at a deposition several months earlier. Faircloth then asked the witness, "Were you lying then or are you lying now?"

The witness responded, "I'm lying now."

LAW AND POLITICS

A young lawyer, Jimmy Kynes, was a key campaign worker during the election of Farris Bryant as Governor of Florida. Kynes then became the new governor's administrative assistant. Months later a vacancy occurred in the office of Attorney General. Governor Bryant appointed Kynes to that position to serve until the next election.

Mr. Earl decided to challenge Kynes in that election and asked Daddy to serve as his state campaign treasurer. I was a college student at the time but became actively involved in that campaign.

Kynes tried to make political gains by emphasizing that Faircloth had practiced law with former U. S. Senator Claude Pepper, considered by many in Florida as very liberal. Mr. Earl's published response was, "I practiced law with Claude Pepper, not politics. My opponent practiced politics with Farris Bryant and law with practically nobody."

POINTING FINGER

Campaigning in North Florida, Mr. Earl saw a friend he had not seen for several years and noticed that the friend's right index finger was missing. Mr. Earl commented that he had not seen him since the accident. The friend said, "That was no accident. That was the finger that pulled the lever for Claude Kirk for Governor and I wanted to make sure that it did not happen again".

Several years later I was speaking for a civic club in Chiefland and told that Faircloth story about the missing finger. Later in the meeting a guest was making his presentation when I noticed that his right index finger was missing. Immediately after the meeting I went over to make sure that I had not offended him. He held up both hands showing that the index finger had been severed from each hand and commented, "Don't worry about it. I voted twice."

LAW SCHOOL

Law School helps to prepare future lawyers in many different ways. The student learns how to research law, analyze cases, write legal briefs and develop skills as an advocate. The interaction between the students as well as the students and professors help to develop mental toughness and sharpness. Having and honing a sense of humor helps a student and lawyer to relieve the tremendous stress that seems to be a necessary part of training and of life.

A SAD STORY

When I arrived at Vanderbilt University to begin law school in the fall of 1965, reservations had been made for a place in a graduate student dormitory. I was aware that I would have a roommate but not knowing the person who would share my living space caused some apprehension mixed with excitement. Soon one of the most memorable characters to ever come into my life was introduced as my new roommate.

W. Brasington VanLandingham was from New England, the son of a lawyer and he drove a white Corvette convertible. The Corvette was sometimes parked in the legal parking spaces but other times in loading zones, on sidewalks or other such places he determined convenient. "Brass" collected parking tickets with the same enthusiasm that some collected green stamps in that day.

In each class Brass sat front and center during his three years in law school. During the orientation classes his hand was in the air, often waving to get the professor's attention. He didn't ask a lot of questions but he did try to supplement the education of his classmates by providing additional information or pointing out errors and inadequacies of the professors. As my Grandpa Callaway said of a Florida politician, "He recommended himself highly."

About the third day of orientation I joined a group of law students gathered in the hallway between classes. Various comments were being made about Brass who had made himself the center of attention in all of the classes.

"Did you hear what he said to Dean Wade?"

Another commented, "What about correcting Professor Patterson yesterday?"

A third student said, "Not only that but what do you think of those bright plaid sport coats he always wears?"

At that point I chimed in, "Not only that, but he is my roommate."

While I was expecting one or more students to apologize thinking they may have offended me, Mike, in his slow Georgia drawl, looked over at me and consoled, "Is that right? That's the saddest story I've ever heard."

BIRD'S EYE VIEW

During the first semester, Professor Patterson asked whether anyone in class was familiar with a certain legal concept. The only one to raise a hand indicating knowledge of that subject matter was my roommate. The professor kept looking around the room as if he hoped he could call on someone other than VanLandingham. Seeing no other hand raised, he reluctantly allowed Brass to expound.

In spite of his own high opinion of himself, most of us had agreed that Brass was a very intelligent young man. His response reflected that intelligence as he explained the legal concept while throwing in a few of his favorite terms such as e.g., i.e. and viz-a-viz.

Professor Patterson seemed to be impressed with his answer but still could not resist taking a shot. "There class, you have a bird's eye view of the matter. Notice that I did not say a bird brain's view."

The class roared. Brass was indignant.

ACUTE HEARING

The youngest member of the faculty wanted to be feared as a really tough professor. Les Hopeful, a student with a slight speech impediment, was seated in the rear of the classroom and was called on by Professor Bogus to recite a case. When Les stood up he started with a slight stammer and was not speaking loudly enough to suit Bogus.

"Speak up Mr. Hopeful. We can't hear you!"

With considerably more volume than before, Les responded, "I can hear you fine, sir."

His classmates cheered their approval.

MEAL TIME

A few of us law students would often leave the law library in late afternoon to get something to eat. On one such occasion, Brass was seated nearby and someone suggested I invite him to come along.

When I approached and asked if he would like to join us for dinner he seemed startled. Looking at his watch Brass exclaimed, "Five o'clock? That's when the servants eat!"

In spite of his pomposity we did learn to like the guy...some.

STUDY HABITS

Flannagan and I roomed together my second year in law school. During those days it was easier for me to get up early to study than to stay up past midnight. As I got ready for bed one night I told him I would be up early to study.

Flannagan indicated that he would continue to read awhile. "If I'm still studying when you get up don't wake me."

BRISTOL BUS

My first law school examination was in Torts (not a dessert), the study of negligence law. It seemed horribly traumatic to many of us.

When I inquired of my classmate Charles Flannagan what he thought of the test, his answer indicated a fatalistic acceptance that his law school days were over. "I was just thinking about asking someone to take me to the bus station so I could buy a ticket to Bristol."

Flannagan survived that test and is now a circuit judge in Bristol, Virginia.

WHAT REALLY HAPPENED?

Criminal law was one of the most interesting subjects for study, especially with professor Karl Warden.

At the beginning of one class period, Professor Warden stepped up to the lectern and waited for the students to settle down. Most quickly seated themselves and became quiet. John, a student on the front row continued standing and appeared to be looking for something in his brief case. The professor cleared his throat; the student ignored him. Directing a comment at John the professor urged him to be seated. When the student continued to disregard him, Warden approached the young man from the rear and placed a hand on his shoulder. John turned around quickly landing a solid punch to the jaw of Professor Warden who then fell to the floor.

John ran up one aisle and out of the classroom. Warden rose holding a bloody handkerchief to his nose and started up the other aisle to exit the room. When he was two-thirds of the way up the aisle most of the previously stunned students began to realize that the incident had been staged and began applauding.

Professor Warden returned to the lectern and instructed each of us to write down what we saw happen. The foregoing account is what I thought had occurred but each student had a different story. The point was well made that eyewitness testimony can vary greatly and is not necessarily the best evidence for determining truth.

FEELING TALL

One of my favorite professors also served as my faculty advisor. Professor Elliott Cheatham was semi-retired at Vanderbilt after having taught for many years at the Columbia University School of Law in New York. He authored several books, a large number of law review articles and had been greatly honored for his contributions to the legal profession.

When I went to him for counsel he made me feel important. Discussing my senior paper, this elderly distinguished professor told me he would like to use some of my ideas in his next book.

Professor Cheatham was such an inspiration to me that I would come out of his office feeling five and a half feet tall.

CONSTITUTING A PUN

One of my best friends in law school, Bill Lebo, had a quick wit and was the prince of puns.

As we discussed the Youngstown Steel case in Constitutional Law class, the professor recounted that the United States Supreme Court ruled that President Truman did not have the constitutional authority to seize the steel mills during the Korean War in the early 1950's. The war, of course, was over by the time the court ruled on it but it did establish a legal precedent. The President could not by executive order legally take over a private business.

Lebo leaned over and whispered to me, "The Court had come to bury seizure and not to praise it."

HELPFUL CLASSMATES

Professor Hartman was referred to as Professor Heartless by many of us. He enjoyed scaring the dickens out of young law students when calling on them to recite cases in class. Those pointed and loaded questions helped to develop the legal minds of the survivors.

Hartman called on Ed Harris for a case but Harris was totally unprepared. The professor's response would have intimidated some of the boldest students but Harris seemed to take it in stride. The next day, Lebo asked another student, Ed Culver, why he had not come to the rescue of his classmate when Hartman put him on the spot.

Culver questioned, "Why me?"

Lebo quipped, "You know two Eds are better than one."

As Culver grimaced and walked away Lebo remarked, "He'll never reCulver from that one."

33

TO SHAFT OR NOT TO SHAFT

While Lebo was the best he was not the only punster in law school. Our Contracts professor told the class about a suit being filed to complain that an engine part was not delivered in accordance with the terms of the contract. "This is the only case I know of in which the Plaintiff complained that he didn't get the shaft."

TALKING SHELLFISH

Most law students at Vanderbilt, including me, gradually moved from fear to respect for Professor Hartman. His unusual style and unique expressions sometimes petrified and at other times entertained his students.

One classmate when called upon was so scared he could not utter a word. Hartman demanded, "Quit making noises like a clam. Speak up!"

WHEN TO TAKE ACTION

A student seated on the front row waved his hand frantically to get the attention of the professor. "What is it, Mr. Mirin?"

"I just wanted to make a comment about that last case."

Hartman responded, "Just to make a comment? Don't ever wave your hand in my face again like that...unless my fly is open. In that case, I would appreciate it."

MORE THAN ONE WAY

During a visit to his office to discuss some of my career objectives and various options that may be available for reaching them, Mr. Hartman said, "There are more ways to choke a dog than on melted butter."

Frankly, I had not even thought of that one.

EVALUATION OF EDUCATION

Critical of the way a lawyer had handled one of the cases we were discussing in class, Professor Hartman said, "The Plaintiff's lawyer must have received his law degree while shaking hands with the postman."

THIN ARGUMENT

A student had been asked to tell what arguments he would use under a certain set of facts presented by Professor Hartman. Obviously not impressed with that student's response, Hartman declared, "Your argument has the substance of the shadow of an emaciated sparrow."

THE RUNT OF THE LITTER

As mentioned in my first book, *I'll Try to Be Short...*, I was born in downtown Chiefland, Florida but my hog pen was only two blocks from City Hall. My rural background allowed me to be acquainted with multiple births of pigs, kittens and puppies. The very smallest animal of the litter is referred to as the runt.

During my Vanderbilt law school days part of the curriculum involved the students being in a "court of appeals" referred to as the moot court program. Mike and A. W. represented the Defendant while Bill and I served as counsel for the Plaintiff. Two second year students, Howard and Fred, served as supervisors of the four first year students. The research, brief writing and oral arguments covered a period of several weeks and the six of us became well acquainted during that time.

Thirty years later I reviewed the careers of the six of us. A. W. Bolt was a senior partner of a successful law firm in Anniston, Alabama and had seriously considered a campaign for Governor. Mike Ahlen became a law professor at the University of North Dakota. Bill Lebo recently retired as general counsel and executive Vice President of the Hilton Hotel Corporation in Beverly Hills, California. Howard Leibengood served as Sergeant at Arms of the United States House of Representatives and later a Washington lobbyist. Fred starred in several Hollywood movies and is better known today as Senator Fred Thompson (R-TN.) playing a prominent role in the leadership of the United States Senate. Howard recently joined his staff.

Based upon that review, I concluded that I am not only physically but also professionally the runt of that litter.

BETTER THAN NONE AT ALL

A Vanderbilt University Symposium featured several prominent personalities of the period. Senator Barry Goldwater of Arizona had lost the election of 1964 to President Lyndon B. Johnson.

The student master of ceremonies introduced Senator Goldwater. He probably meant to say that the Senator was "certainly a man of integrity." What he actually said brought a roar of laughter!

"Senator Goldwater is a man with a certain degree of integrity."

GETTING STARTED

It did not take me long to learn that law school did not prepare me for the practice of law. Some of the most interesting things happened during that first year.

The ability to draft a Complaint did not mean that I would know what to do with it afterward. Finding the courthouse in rural Levy County was not a big problem. Knowing which office to go to and what procedures were required for filing the lawsuit, finding a recorded deed, having a mobile home title transferred and many other basic functions were totally foreign. Some of my former high school classmates who had never gone to college at all were seasoned employees of the Clerk's office. It was rather humiliating to have to ask them, "What do I do now?"

EQUALLY INCOMPETENT

A lawyer in his 80s was still practicing in our area when I began my law practice at the tender age of twenty-six. His advanced age did not cause his incompetence according to courthouse officials and other lawyers who knew him much longer than I did. Examination of abstracts and deeds prepared by him many years before I became a member of the Florida Bar confirmed to me that Mr. Olden had never been considered among the best of our profession. My lack of experience in the law practice and particularly in trial work made me a good match for the incompetence of that lawyer fifty years my senior.

Mr. Olden was into recycling when recycling wasn't cool. Envelopes in which he had received mail were re-used by taping or stapling the end of the envelope. Names and addresses to whom he was sending the letter would appear above his own marked-out name and address. Court pleadings and letters to other attorneys were typed on the backs of old insurance forms he also carefully recycled.

It is not unusual to have difficulty reading the handwriting of a doctor or a lawyer. But trying to make sense of the pleading he filed was nearly impossible because of the illegible type of his crippled manual typewriter. Evidence existed that it had been in sub-par condition for many years....letters that wouldn't strike, numerous cross-outs and crossovers, smudges and other obstacles to clarity.

Mr. Olden filed a lawsuit entitled "Complaint to Quiet Title and for Accounting" relating to property which had been owned by one or more persons who had died many years before. Title would have been considered to be owned by the heirs.

A hearing was held before Judge Murphree on my Motion to Dismiss in which I stated that the Complaint "failed to state a cause of action." This judge seldom spoke above a whisper and the old lawyer probably had difficulty hearing thunder. Criticizing me for my inadequate motion, Judge Murphree said that the rules require a Motion to Dismiss must state "with specificity" the grounds for such motion and he indicated that I clearly had not done that. Mr. Olden did not hear what the judge said even though his hand was cupped over his ear during the entire hearing.

"I don't know whether I should let you argue this Motion since you have not complied with the rule," the judge continued, then paused to consider the matter. "Aahh, go ahead and argue your Motion. It's at least as good as the Complaint."

"IF HE DON'T COME SEE ME..."

One of the senior judges told me about his first experience of campaigning to be elected as Circuit Judge in 1944. He went up on the porch of a small farmhouse in a remote area of the circuit. The woman of the house came to the door. He introduced himself and told her he would like to have her vote for circuit judge.

"Well, since you came to see me I'll probably vote for you. But if you had not come to my house I wouldn't vote for you because I don't vote for nobody that don't come see me."

"You're going to vote for President Roosevelt aren't you?"

"If he don't come see me, I ain't."

JUDICIAL DIPLOMACY

Because circuit judge John Crews was a friend of Earl Faircloth (the family friend referred to earlier who had served in the legislature and as Attorney General for the State of Florida) I felt some comfort in discussing with the judge various opinions of mine relating to political matters. I had made several critical comments about the Governor without considering the fact that Judge Crews had not been elected to the judicial office he held.

In response to my criticism Judge Crews offered, "Much of what you say is true. However, he has made some very fine appointments."

Realizing the error of my ways I humbly but sincerely replied, "Yes, one in particular."

TERRAZZO TERROR

My first law office had two small rooms with extremely hard terrazzo floors. There was a telephone at my desk in one room and a telephone on the secretary's desk in the other room. No hold buttons. Both phones on the same line.

During an office conference with clients my secretary came to the door to tell me that Judge Murphree was on the line and wanted to speak with me. Lacking the confidence that I could impress my clients by talking to a circuit judge in their presence, I got up from my desk to go to the other room. My foot got tangled up in the phone cord, jerked the phone off the desk and onto the terrazzo floor. The crash created tremendous noise in my office and undoubtedly in the ear of the judge.

I apologized to the judge but I don't think he heard me.

LAP ROBES FOR JUDGES?

A project of one women's Sunday school class in our church several years ago was to make lap robes for elderly residents of a nearby nursing home. On one occasion Judge Crews, who was not wearing his judicial robe at the time, could certainly have used a lap robe.

After appearing in court before him on a non-jury matter shortly before noon, the two of us went to a local sundry shop for lunch. Hoping to improve my image with the judge, my case of nerves probably caused me to be more clumsy than usual. As I reached for the salt & pepper I knocked over my glass of Pepsi Cola and the entire contents dumped into the judge's lap.

Expressing my apologies I added, "I guess it's a good thing I don't have to be in court before you this afternoon."

The judge agreed.

HEARING OR HEALING?

A divorce client was anxious to get a Final Judgment entered and did not want to wait several more days for a judge to be available in our county. I called Judge Crews' office and found I could go to nearby Trenton where he was conducting a jury trial in the Gilchrist County Courthouse. The judge told me he would be glad to take a break and have the brief uncontested hearing that was needed in order to set my client free of that marriage.

When we arrived at the courthouse I sat on the back row of the courtroom observing the jury selection process being conducted by the attorneys with very little direct involvement by the judge. While sitting there for twenty or thirty minutes in a rather uncomfortable seat, my right leg went to sleep from my hip through the end of my toes. About that time Judge Crews saw me on the back row and signaled for me to come to the bench. It was not easy but I was able to stand up and move to the aisle, carefully dragging my numb leg as I approached.

The judge informed me that he would declare a recess in a few minutes and would plan to meet with my client, her witness and me for the brief hearing required. Standing at the bench I had been able to move that numb leg around enough to get the circulation going again. I was able to walk back to my seat in the courtroom with the normal gait that my short legs allowed.

If there is a legend that Judge Crews was not only a great jurist but also a faith healer, this true story may explain its origin.

CIRCUIT JUDGE
FAITH HEALER

53

PISTOL PACKING MAMA

In the first few weeks of my private practice, a woman came to my office and retained me to represent her in a divorce proceeding. Mrs. Packer had five or six children, a husband and someone I suspect she liked a whole lot more than her husband. The husband's attorney was much more aggressive than the one the wife had retained. A hearing was set in Gainesville before Judge Crews to determine whether the Complaint for Divorce would be granted and to determine which of the competing parents would be awarded custody of the young children.

A week before the hearing my client met with me in my office to discuss strategy. When I told her that there was no guarantee that she would win custody of the children she reacted angrily, "My husband is not fit to have those children! I'll kill him before I'll let him have them!"

I advised her not to even think about such drastic action and really thought that she was not serious about her intent to eliminate the other parent if the judge awarded custody to him.

The day of the hearing Mrs. Packer reportedly made comments to acquaintances in the community that she would "shoot everybody in the courtroom" if she did not get custody of her children. Those comments were passed on to her husband and his lawyer.

During the hearing my client testified as to why she should be granted a divorce and that she would be the proper parent to care for the children. Her sister and mother testified on her behalf. Mr. Packer and his girlfriend told the court that my client was not a good mother, that she worked in a bar until the early morning hours and sometimes allowed her children to serve drinks in the bar. They testified that she allowed the children to play in the highway and did not provide adequate food and clothing for them.

Judge Crews, after hearing the testimony, announced that he would grant the wife's Complaint for Divorce on the ground of "extreme cruelty" but that he was awarding custody of the children "at least temporarily" to the father.

Mrs. Packer stood up, pushed her chair back from the table, took one very deep breath and collapsed on the floor rolling under the table. Her now ex-husband jumped up saying that he would try to help her because she had previously experienced similar fainting spells.

Counsel for Mr. Packer came around the table and as he reached down for her handbag asked, "Do you have any smelling salts or other medicine you take for these spells?"

Although she gave no response he pulled her handbag from under her body and placed it on the table. He opened the bag, reached in and pulled out a dirty washcloth with something wrapped up in it. Handing it to me he somewhat flippantly said, "Here Luther, stick this in your pocket."

Standing there stunned, probably praying and nearly crying, I took the object he handed me and put it in my coat pocket. It certainly felt like a pistol and the weight made me list. I walked into a small passageway between the hearing room and the judge's office to which he had retreated when Mrs. Packer fainted.

The other lawyer suggested that we show the judge what he had taken from her handbag. Judge Crews opened the dirty washcloth and lying in his hand was a .22-caliber revolver. Examining the pistol he found a live round in the chamber and one additional cartridge. The fact that there was not enough ammunition to shoot everyone in the courtroom gave me little comfort.

This dramatic turn of events had taken place on the third floor of the courthouse with the Sheriff's office on the ground floor of the same building. Judge Crews picked up the phone, called the Sheriff and demanded, "This is Judge Crews and I want a Deputy up here right now!" The respect for his office was intensified by his commanding voice.

A Deputy appeared in the hearing room almost instantly. I was so shaken that the instructions of the judge made an indelible impression on my mind. I believe that the following is an exact quotation of what Judge Crews ordered. "Mr. Deputy Sheriff, I direct that you take this white female into your custody and confine her in the common jail of Alachua County until a time certain when she shall be brought before me, to show cause, if any she may have, why she should not be held in direct contempt of this court!"

Mrs. Packer turned to me and asked, "You're my lawyer. What am I supposed to do?"

What followed was some of the best legal advice I ever gave a client. "If Judge Crews says for you to go with the Deputy, you'd better do it."

A hearing was held the next day and Judge Crews ordered her to be kept in jail until examined by two court-appointed psychiatrists. After about ten days their report indicated no homicidal intent and the judge released her from jail.

In less than a year her ex-husband was tired of taking care of the children and let her have them.

That was the last child custody case I ever handled. In fact, serious consideration was given to taking my shingle down on the very day of the pistol packing mama incident.

STREET TALK

Most of the judges I have had any dealings with have consistently maintained "judicial decorum" or a sense of dignity about the office of judge. There were exceptions.

A woman in late middle age had been abandoned by her husband several years earlier but never had gone to the trouble of having the marriage dissolved. When she finally came to me for a Dissolution of Marriage the proceeding was filed and a hearing set before one of the circuit judges. Brief testimony was presented by my client and her witness. The judge determined that the legal requirements were met and signed the proposed Order I had prepared. As he completed his signature, he looked up at the woman and announced, "As they say on the streets of Gainesville...'you is split'!"

CHASM SPASM

My client had done some tractor work in clearing land for a couple who lived in another county about an hour and a half away from my office. The property owners failed to pay my client for those services and did not repay a loan of a few hundred dollars. When the debtors did not respond to my demand letters on behalf of my client, a suit was filed in their county to obtain a judgment for the money owed.

Neither the husband nor the wife filed any response to the complaint and under the rules of the court a default judgment was entered against each of them. The matter was set for a hearing which I attended with an Affidavit from my client stating that services had been rendered and payment had not been received.

The Defendants (both husband and wife) had been personally served by the Sheriff with a Notice of the action but neither filed any responsive pleading nor attended the hearing. In spite of that fact the judge refused to enter the order I requested. His main hang-up seemed to be that the check for the loan had been made out to the husband only. Judge Chafe would only enter a judgment against the husband unless I amended my complaint, filed it and had the Defendants personally served again.

I argued that the land was owned by both and that the money as well as the land clearing service was for the benefit of both Defendants. They each had ample opportunity to object to the claim. But Judge Chafe held firm saying, "I can't bridge that chasm." He required a choice of obtaining a judgment against the husband only or, in effect, starting over.

Knowing that a judgment against the husband only would be difficult to collect because all property was jointly owned, my only reasonable choice was to try to act calm. Even though it meant a few weeks delay, I chose to amend the complaint so that judgment would be against both Defendants. An amended complaint was filed but not before dealing with some irritation and anger over the judge's ruling.

About the only satisfying moment I had on that court date was on my way home. As I approached a country crossroad, a large rattlesnake slithered onto the highway. I was able to retire it with my car (pun intended). In reporting on that event to some of my friends, I told them that I probably was angry enough to have dealt with the rattlesnake by hand!

"ORE TENUS" or **BE STUPID**

Not all lawyers want to trample and humiliate opposing counsel. During those early learning days I was in a hearing representing one of the Defendants in a multi-party lawsuit. As the facts were being revealed along with my ignorance in the practice, one of the older lawyers kindly suggested to the judge, "It seems to me, Your Honor, that it would have been proper if Mr. Beauchamp had filed a Motion for dismissal of his client from the suit.

An equally kind judge responded, "I see no reason why I could not accept that Motion Ore Tenus."

Remembering just enough of my law school experience with Latin terms, I was fairly confident that Ore Tenus meant a spoken or oral motion. "I make that Motion."

"It's granted," the judge said with a smile.

NOT SO FANCY FOOTWORK

My first Worker Compensation case involved a claim by my client who had broken an ankle when she slipped on a wet floor in the restaurant kitchen where she was employed.

During presentation of our case, I asked her questions which allowed her to testify that she had undergone surgery three different times on her ankle and was still unable to work. Mrs. Bream testified that she had made an effort to go back to work but because of some surgery in January of that year she still had not been able to return to work.

Later I realized that I had not studied the medical records closely enough to be prepared for what happened next.

The insurance company's lawyer cross-examined my client and asked about the different surgeries she had endured on her ankle. Then he asked about the surgery she had in January. "Was that surgery on your ankle?"

"No. It was a female operation. It didn't have nuthin' to do with my foot."

At that moment this short lawyer got a little bit shorter.

NOT THE GAME THEY WERE HUNTING

As mentioned earlier, the study of criminal law was one of the more interesting subjects but it did not take me long to learn that I did not like the actual practice of criminal law.

An old story a friend used to rib me with was that someone had stopped in our small town and asked, "Is there a criminal lawyer in this place?"

The response was, "We think so but we haven't been able to prove it on him yet."

One of my few cases involving criminal law was when I represented three men who had been arrested in neighboring Dixie County for hunting violations. They had been caught while riding horses after midnight in woods where deer were often seen. In their possession were guns and lights.

They retained me to represent them even though neither they nor their attorney could think of any good defense to the charges. No one I consulted was aware that anyone had ever served jail time for a hunting violation in that county. My clients were not charged with killing game or even shooting at any. In fact they assured me they had not even seen a deer that night. Believing the matter could be resolved in a short time with the only consequences being a fine and probation we appeared in open court and entered a plea of "no contest" meaning that my clients did not admit guilt but had chosen not to defend the charges. They were at the mercy of the court but on that day the court had very little.

The courtroom was crowded with hunting club members and other sportsmen who had decided it was now time to crack down on illegal hunting (that does not mean looking for sick birds). Their presence had a greater influence on the judge than my urging that no jail time be required.

Each man was sentenced to pay a fine of $300 and to serve 10 days in the county jail. Two of the three men had no prior arrests and had young families and good jobs that would be affected by their confinement. We were all in shock as the judge turned them over to a deputy to begin their incarceration that very day. The court adjourned.

Desperately trying to find help in this time of need I turned to the statute book and carefully read the state law under which they were convicted. Finding a ray of hope I went to the judge's office and asked for permission to speak with him.

I read the law to the judge pointing out that it provided upon conviction of a violation a defendant would be subject to "a fine not to exceed $500 or imprisonment in the county jail for a term not to exceed one year." My emphasis was that the statute clearly stated that the sentence could be a fine or imprisonment. The judge had sentenced them to both and I suggested as respectfully as I knew how that an appeal must be considered if he allowed the sentence to remain as announced in the court-room.

The judge asked me to let him read the language of the law. He agreed that there could be a question of whether he had authority to fine and imprison. The three men were brought back in before the judge. He told them he would suspend the jail time but if they were charged with any violation of the law in Dixie County within the next 12 months they would have to serve the 10 days in jail plus any other sentence imposed for the second offense.

Each of my clients not only promised to avoid violating any laws in that county but also assured the judge they had no plans to ever return to Dixie County, day or night.

THE BEST THINGS

Our Worker's Compensation judge in the '70s was Judge Akins of Trenton. While discussing the importance of lawyers being paid for their services, the judge quipped, "The best things in life are fee."

Being paid is important to lawyers and everyone else but the longer I live the more I realize that the best **things** in life are not **things**.

THE BEST THINGS IN LIFE ARE...

NAMES TO REMEMBER

During my college days at FSU a girl who was active in the Baptist Student Union was named Merry Christmas. On a sign-up sheet for a student retreat she had added her name to the list of other students planning to attend. Beside her name another student wrote, "Happy New Year!"

Professors in law school enjoyed creating names for situations to test student knowledge or analytical ability. One such story featured a self-righteous character the professor named "I. M. Godlike."

In my law practice the most interesting client names I remember (and these are not made-up) were Stormy Knight, Anita Pickel and Wauna B. Ritch.

SATISFACTION OF MARRIAGE?

Handling real estate transactions has been a significant part of my practice for more than 30 years. We often encounter preparation of Mortgages securing Promissory Notes. Then when the Mortgage is paid in full, the people being paid execute a document entitled Satisfaction of Mortgage. That instrument is then recorded in the public records to show that the Mortgage no longer will count as a lien against the property.

Early in my practice one of my divorce clients complained about the infidelity of her husband. She seemed more concerned, however, that his extra-marital relations had resulted in transmission of a disease to her. Smugly she stated, "When I found out who the other woman was, I went over to her house and I beat on her 'til I was satisfied!"

INFORMATION, PLEASE

When the phone rings at my house after midnight I usually think there must be an emergency or some other bad news.

A friend of mine in the logging business told me he got a call at 4 a.m. and stumbled to the phone. The party on the line said, "I hope I didn't wake you up."

His response was, "Nope, not yet."

I felt much the same when I received a call after midnight from one of my divorce clients. He must have been trying to drown his sorrows with the benefit of a few bottles that Saturday night. The purpose of his call was to find out what time his hearing would be on the following Thursday.

It seemed to me that he could have waited until Monday or Tuesday during office hours. I know it would have fit my schedule better.

CITY FATHERS?

In the early 1970's I agreed to serve as attorney for the City of Cedar Key, a small island community along the Gulf Coast about 30 miles from my hometown.

The Honorable Justice James C. Adkins, Jr. was serving on the Florida Supreme Court at that time but had earlier practiced law in Gainesville, Florida. He also maintained a home in Cedar Key. When Justice Adkins learned that I had become the new City Attorney he made this suggestion to me. "Most of the people down there want to do things differently than the rest of the country anyway. You should tell them to knock out the Number 4 bridge and raise their own flag!"

Although there were and still are many very nice people in Cedar Key, I learned what the justice was talking about as I discovered the attitudes of many relating to legal authority. Some of those with authority seemed to think that the laws did not apply to them. Those who had some legal authority frequently wanted to assert more than was given. . .

THE $25 PER MONTH JUDGE

During my tenure as City Attorney in Cedar Key several different persons served as the municipal judge. There was no legal requirement at that time that the judge have any legal training, experience or ability to hold that position. The court met about twice a month and the salary for the judge was $25 whether he earned it or not.

Not many people were eager to take the job but the city council would usually be able to persuade someone to serve. When the former judge resigned, the vacancy was filled on the spot by a commercial fisherman who happened to be a spectator at the council meeting.

It was not long until Judge Fisher created no small stir by his demonstration of pride in his new position. The city clerk called me and said that some of the city councilmen wanted to know if the city charter would allow them to fire the judge they had just hired. I learned that the complaints about Judge Fisher included:

1) While walking along the street Judge Fisher noticed two citizens arguing about whether one of them could build a dock in the location he had chosen. One of them complained that it was on the city right-of-way and not on the land belonging to the man attempting to build the dock. The judge had given an "eyeball survey" and ruled in favor of the landowner saying that the location was on the landowners' property and he could build there. A legal ruling on the location of property lines was not within the jurisdiction of the city court even if the matter had been properly filed.

2) The city policeman had left the police car unlocked one night with the police record book on the front seat. A city councilman seeing the situation and thinking that there was a risk that the book would be stolen, took it home for safe keeping. The next morning the councilman called city hall to report that he had the record book and would bring it down later that day. When the judge arrived to hold city court the policeman reported that the councilman had the book and he could not present his cases. Judge Fisher then issued a written Order threatening fine or jail time for the councilman. This was not within the power of his office.

After studying the Charter I advised the city council that it would be within their authority to dismiss the judge.

Judge Fisher went to the University of Florida and obtained the services of the Legal Aid clinic to fight his battles for him at no cost. They persuaded a circuit judge to issue an Order directing the City Council to follow the Administrative Procedure Act. The Order required that he be reinstated and a hearing be held to determine whether there was sufficient cause to dismiss him from the position.

The circuit judge refused to require the city to pay the costs of having a court reporter and some other requests made by Judge Fisher's counsel. The parties were able to reach an agreement to pay the judge an amount equal to 3 months' salary (a total of $75) in exchange for his "voluntary" resignation. There was no further court action.

IT'S WORTH $5

In another municipality in our area, a city commissioner who was assigned the responsibility for overseeing the municipal water services had allowed the water department to turn off the water supply to a delinquent customer's home. She was the daughter of a fellow commissioner and had received the proper notice and warning required by the city ordinance. Because the water had been disconnected it cost her a $5 fee to have it turned on again plus payment of the delinquent account.

At the next commission meeting there ensued a 30-minute argument over whether she should be required to pay the $5 or whether the commissioner had acted improperly.

Deciding that half an hour was enough debate on that issue, the City Attorney rose from his chair. Before leaving the room he opened his wallet and quietly placed a $5 bill on the table.

DON'T ASK

Sometime during my tenure as attorney for the Board of County Commissioners, a question came up about whether the county could have its road department put a truckload or two of limerock on a road inside a private cemetery. I knew it was something that the Commissioners wanted to do because it would help some very concerned constituents. I also knew that there were legal restraints relating to using county funds, materials or employees to improve private property.

One Commissioner turned to me and asked, "Counselor, what do you think about that?"

With very little hesitation I replied, "If you want to do it, don't ask me."

WHERE'S THE BATHROOM?

An agreement for deed is a contract by which a real estate owner agrees to sell certain property to a buyer but retains legal title to the property until the final payment is made.

My client had sold some property using an Agreement for Deed and came to me because the buyer had quit making payments on the contract. I sent a letter to the woman who was supposed to be making the payments demanding that she either bring all of the payments current, pay the contract in full or sign a Quitclaim Deed releasing all of her interest in the property back to my client.

A response came from the buyer in the form of a letter. The greeting in the letter was "Hello Mr. R. Luther Beauchamp." She then told me in the letter that the Agreement for Deed had said that one of the things my client would do after the papers were signed was to complete construction of the house by adding a bathroom to the property. She then stated, "I don't see no bathroom!"

When I read the contract and confirmed that it did require my client to complete the construction my optimism about our case diminished. I figured that the bathroom was not there if the buyer "don't see no bathroom."

CRIMES OF ALL SIZES

Cases before the judge were being heard in chambers behind the courtroom. Attorneys who had hearings scheduled waited in the courtroom until called.

A young man opened the doors of the main courtroom and asked, "Is this where the small crimes court meets?"

He probably meant "small claims" but may have been feeling so guilty that "crime" seemed like a better word.

WHOSE HOGS?

There was a lawyer in Gainesville by the name of Sigsbee Scruggs. He'd had an illustrious career and many stories circulated about him, some of which were probably true.

One such story concerned his representation of a man charged with the crime of stealing hogs. The jury returned a verdict of guilty and the Defendant was upset. Turning to his lawyer the convicted hog thief said, "If I'd had a good lawyer I would have won this case!"

Scruggs responded, "If those had been your hogs you would have won this case."

VEGETABLES IN COURT

My brother was a circus judge...I mean a circuit judge. For almost 20 years prior to his appointment to the circuit court bench, W.O. served as our county judge. Before that he had served as an Assistant Attorney General in Tallahassee.

During the time he worked for the Attorney General's office he handled a variety of cases, many involving citizens who were representing themselves and had no attorney filing documents on their behalf.

There is a pleading entitled "Motion to Quash" which is provided for under the rules of the court. That motion is appropriate when you are asking the court to strike a portion of the pleadings or to dismiss the lawsuit altogether.

W.O. received in the mail a copy of a document which the other party had filed entitled "Motion to Squash."

There is an old adage, "He who is his own lawyer has a fool for a client." That's not always a true statement. There is enough evidence, however, that in many cases it **is** true.

STRANGE LEGAL TERMS

People trying to use unfamiliar words sometimes come up with previously unused terms as their substitute.

An abstract is a record of previous transactions affecting title to real estate. It usually lists deeds, mortgages, judgments and other documents with the recording information as to where they may be found in the public records. More than one client has reported, "I have an abstract deed for my property." I still don't know what that is.

A warranty deed contains the covenant or guarantee of the one signing the deed that the title is clear except for those things already disclosed as exceptions, if any. The quit-claim deed, unlike the warranty makes no promise of clear title but merely is evidence that the one signing it will no longer claim any interest in the property. Mistakenly, many clients have referred to a "quick-claim" deed when they mean quit-claim. Maybe it's just a little faster than the other one.

Among my favorite misuses of legal terms is when a judge has released a defendant without requiring a money deposit or cash bond. This is referred to as a recognizance bond, being released because the court is satisfied the defendant will appear in court when required and could be recognized by the law enforcement officers. Some have said, "he was released on his own 'reconnaissance'."

WHO'S READY?

In another case W.O. handled for the Attorney General's office the other party was again not represented by counsel. Wanting to move the case along and get it completed, W.O. filed a "Notice that Case is Ready for Trial" and requested the clerk to schedule a hearing before the judge. If the other party does not agree, the usual response is to file a motion to strike the notice or file an objection to setting the matter for trial.

In this case the other party filed a document entitled "Notice that Case Is **Not** Ready for Trial."

GENEROUS LAWYERS

During my practice with Joseph E. Smith in Bronson several interesting events took place.

Joe was representing a Miami developer who was attempting to acquire various tracts of land in the Bronson area for development. Much confusion existed about where some of the boundary lines were located and whether the titles were clear. Defects in titles on property in that area were due to errors in legal descriptions, failure to settle estates of persons long deceased and a variety of other reasons.

Mr. Urban had negotiated with the heirs of a deceased person to sign a Quitclaim deed for any property owned by that estate in the town of Bronson. That is a rather vague legal description but it would solve the problem if that family had an interest in any property within the city limits. The client asked that the Deed be made to Joseph E. Smith and R. Luther Beauchamp until he could determine how he wanted to take title to the property. As an accommodation, we agreed to accept the Quitclaim deeds in our names.

The problem arose when Mr. Urban requested that we execute a Quitclaim deed conveying the property we were holding over to his new corporation. Parties on the original Quitclaim deed to us had fully intended to release any rights they had to property in the town of Bronson but we very carelessly used the same legal description in the Quitclaim to Mr. Urban's new corporation. A deed from Joseph E. Smith and R. Luther Beauchamp releasing all of our rights to any lands owned in the town of Bronson had the effect of giving away our law office!

After much embarrassment and humiliation, accompanied by good-natured ribbing by our very good friend who owned a title company, we were able to persuade Mr. Urban to have his corporation give us back our law office.

LAWYERS DON'T KNOW IT ALL

I have actually had some people call me at home and tell me that they called to ask legal questions there because they did not want to bother me at my office. Some probably call me at home because they think that they would only have to pay a fee if they call me during office hours.

One such call to my home was a man who wanted an interpretation of a contract that I had never seen. He asked if the other party could enforce that contract and make him do certain things. I told him I would have to read the contract before I could answer those questions. To the next question I responded, "I don't know."

In apparent astonishment the caller queried, "You don't know? You're a lawyer, ain't ya?"

THE REAL MEANING

One of my earliest law partners was Joseph E. Smith who is now our county judge. He has mellowed some and developed much more patience than he exhibited in his early years.

Our firm represented a Savings and Loan Association preparing necessary documents and handling loan transactions. Joe became very efficient at the task of getting the documents executed by the Borrowers. His efficiency probably grew out of impatience and the knowledge that we were being paid a very small fee for each transaction. He needed to get on to other things.

At one such closing Joe spread the papers out on the table and told the Borrowers, "Sign here, here, here, here, here, here and here" as he pointed to the lines for signatures.

The wife, who had already managed to irritate him with a lot of questions prior to the signing objected. "I am not going to sign anything until I know what these papers say."

Very firmly Joe informed her, "They say that if you don't sign where I tell you to, you are not going to get the money!"

With that very clear explanation she and her husband signed all of the necessary papers.

QUALIFIED TO SPEAK

My very good friend and former law partner, Judge Joseph E. Smith, has endured more comments about his bald head than I have about my lack of height. He has heard them all and handles it with a good sense of humor.

"God showed Joe a special favor by giving him one face and clearing land for another."

Joe proudly responded, "Grass won't grow on a busy street."

Back came the retort, "And it won't grow up through concrete either."

Once when I had neglected to see my barber longer than usual and my hair was hanging over my ears, Joe asked in the presence of a few other folks, "Luther, when are you going to do something about your hair?"

Turning to another man in the office I asked, "Would you let a barefooted man tell you what kind of shoes to wear?"

IDENTIFY YOURSELF, PLEASE

A few years ago I was introduced as "the senior partner in his city's largest law firm." The Master of Ceremonies then added, "His nephew is the other lawyer." That introduction was accurate because at the time my nephew and I made up the only law firm in our town with more than one lawyer.

Brett was appointed by the court to represent an indigent defendant in a drug case. The accused was being held in the county jail. Brett went over to talk with him and find out what evidence the prosecutor intended to present in support of the charges. Part of the evidence included a surveillance video in which the accused's criminal activity was reported to have been captured on film. A possible defense to consider in such cases would be one of mistaken identity. A defendant could require the prosecutor to prove beyond reasonable doubt that the person shown in the video was actually the person now charged with the crime.

As Brett and the defendant watched the video along with a representative of the Sheriff's department, the accused made the job of prosecution much easier by exclaiming as he pointed to the video screen, "That's me right there!"

EVERYONE COUNTS

A local bank was willing to make a loan to the young man only if his father co-signed or guaranteed the loan. The original loan was for $20,000 to be paid back in 6 months. Mr. Stuckee signed with his son guaranteeing payment.

At the end of the 6 months a significant amount of the loan remained unpaid and the bank allowed the son to sign extending the loan another 6 months. Once again the bank extended the loan yet another 6 months. Each extension was made with only Junior signing and no notice was ever given to the father.

Two years from the original signing of the note, the son's business was in trouble and he filed for bankruptcy. The bank notified Mr. Stuckee that there was a balance of $8,500 remaining on the note and they looked to him for payment. He refused.

A suit was filed by the bank against the father for the payment of the note and he came to me to represent him. Knowing the temperament of this client and the possibility that his defense would not be successful, I persuaded him that more experienced counsel should join me in defending the matter. We prepared for trial and thought we had the law and the facts on our side.

LAUNDERED FUNDS ?

Judge Dozer did hear some of the arguments between periods of sleep. His ruling ignored what we believed was the clear meaning of a statute. That law would have required the bank to have notified Mr. Stuckee if any extension of the debt exceeded more than an additional 6 months from the original due date. Our client and his attorneys were very upset about the court's ruling and felt confident that an appeal would be successful.

An appeal bond had to be posted. In order to avoid having to post a cash bond, Mr. Stuckee persuaded two of his friends, local businessmen, to sign as guarantors on an appeal bond.

Appellate briefs were filed by us for the father and by the bank's counsel. We waited a few months for a decision from the First District Court of Appeals. When the decision came down from Tallahassee, there was no written opinion, only the words "per curiam affirmed." That means that the three judges agreed to allow the trial court judge's ruling to stand without rendering any kind of opinion. (I sometimes think that Latin term may mean, "None of us had time to read this case.")

With some difficulty, we convinced Mr. Stuckee that it had now become necessary for him to pay off the judgment which with accrued interest, court costs and attorney fees exceeded $11,000. A time was set to meet at the office of one of the kind friends of our client who had signed his appeal bond.

His friend was present in the office along with counsel for the bank when I arrived. The group had to wait several minutes for my client to arrive. With a very unhappy countenance and a large laundry bag in his hands, Mr. Stuckee came through the door and began dumping $1 bills onto the desk. When the bag was empty he turned to me and said, "I'm goin' home but I want you to stay here until they are satisfied that they have all of their money and you get a Satisfaction of Judgment for me."

Embarrassed and intimidated, I replied, "Yes sir, I will."

About five minutes after Mr. Stuckee left, an employee of the business came to the door and asked, "Does anyone in here own a small yellow Datsun?"

"What about it?" asked the banks' attorney with obvious concern.

"Mr. Stuckee just backed into it in the parking lot. He brought us his name, address, telephone number and insurance company name and told us he was going home because he didn't feel well."

Two hours later the counting was done. The money was all there with half of a one dollar bill extra. I carry that memento in my wallet to this day.

EVEN EARLY CAN BE TOO LATE

On my way home for lunch recently I became aware of an ambulance behind me with lights flashing. My lawyer instinct has taught me that I must let an ambulance get ahead of me in order for me to chase it. I followed the emergency vehicle to its destination very near the turn off for my home.

Only a few people were at the scene but to my surprise another lawyer was already there.

Actually, neither he nor I had any intention of soliciting legal business. My primary areas of practice are estate planning, estate administration and real estate transactions. The other lawyer's home was the closest to the accident scene and he is a retired bank trust officer who has never practiced law in our county.

ORGANIZED ESTATE PLANNING

It is usually my practice to allow clients to tell me in their own words what they want to accomplish when establishing a plan to distribute their assets after death. During one of those office conferences, my client explained that he and his wife wanted to own everything together as long as they both lived and then "when one of us dies, it all goes to the longest liver."

I understood that he was referring to the survivor of the two of them and not to the length of an internal organ.

That event reminded me of a story (as most everything does) about a woman who said she was going to ask the church to pray for her gallbladder. A friend told her that she thought it was fine to ask the church to pray for her health but that it was not appropriate to request prayer for a single organ in the body.

The ailing woman responded, "I don't see why I can't ask them to pray for my gallbladder. Last Sunday the preacher prayed for all of the loose livers in the community."

SPLINTERS IN MOUTH

My cousin, Greg, who was my law partner for several years, represented a party in a real estate transaction in another county. When the closing agent indicated it was time for the Buyer to pay the purchase price and his share of the closing costs, Mr. Chips counted out a large sum of money in small bills creating a sizable stack of cash on the table.

Wanting to add a little humor to the occasion, Greg facetiously said, "Somebody better close the door. Anybody coming by would think we're dealing with drug money."

Nobody laughed.

After the closing was completed and Greg was alone with his client he learned why his comment was not funny. The client informed him that the other party was the infamous kingpin of drug trafficking in that area. "When you made that comment about the drug money I thought I was going to bite off the end of the table!"

OUT OF SIGHT BUT HEARD

My courtroom appearances have been relatively few over the 30+ years of law practice. Probably because of my "pistol packing mama" case and other unpleasant experiences, I began specializing out of those cases requiring confrontations. Real estate and probate work seldom required me to be in a courtroom.

A rare appearance was made a few years ago when a nonprofit corporation I represented was in court over a salary dispute with a former employee. The judge asked the lawyers to "approach the bench." In order to see me the judge had to lean over the front of the bench.

GO 'NOLES!

A few days later our local newspaper included an article entitled, "Judge Asks for Platform to be Added to Courtroom." The judge was reported to have said he had a "problem talking to some of the shorter lawyers during bench conferences."

My name was not used in the story but it is satisfying to know that I have had impact upon the way justice is carried out in my county courthouse.

Speaking for a civic club in Gainesville, Florida I remembered after a few minutes into my presentation that the club president had provided a foot high stool for me to stand on. Moving the stool in place behind the lectern and taking my place on it, I confessed, "This is much better. Can you see me now?"

A voice from my left responded, "We wondered where you were."

DECISION BY DECIBEL

My current law partner, Michael Koch, will be able to write his own book some day. He has a wonderful sense of humor and a keen legal mind.

During a recent hearing he knew that his client was not in a strong position in relation to the law or the facts. His client believed a former roommate had defrauded him of an interest in some real estate. One theory of recovery was that a business partnership had existed between the man and his friend regarding the property even though legal title was in her name only.

Arguing against a motion to dismiss his client's claim, Mike admitted to the circuit judge, "Your Honor, I can't show you anything that screams partnership."

Judge Cates wryly responded, "Mr. Koch, can you show me something that even whispers partnership?"

About the Author

Luther Beauchamp is a Christian lawyer (those are not mutually exclusive terms) who lives in Chiefland, Florida, the place of his birth. He and Vera, his wife of more than thirty years, have two grown children and enjoy the status of grandparents.

A graduate of Florida State University and the Vanderbilt University School of Law, his law practice is primarily in the area of estate planning and administration and real estate transactions. Beauchamp is active in his church and serves as general counsel for the Florida Baptist Convention.

He is an entertaining and motivating speaker for business, church, civic and school groups, and is a member of the National Speakers Association. Demand for speaking engagements continues to increase each year throughout the Southeast and other areas of the country.

Contact Luther to speak for your group. Call toll-free 1-888-568-6677. See his website at www.lutherbeauchamp.com, email him at legalaugh@aol.com, or write to him at:

P.O. Box 10
Chiefland, FL 32644.

About Cartoonist Joe McKeever

Joe McKeever's coal-mining father, Carl, served as his first art model during childhood days in West Virginia and Alabama. In the evenings, while his tired father napped in front of the radio, Joe drew him. Occasionally, his dad would stir, ask to see the drawing, and comment that "the hairline is too low" or "the ear is too big." Joe would erase, Carl would drift back to sleep, and the drawing lesson continued. Mr. McKeever is now in his 90th year, and Joe is still drawing him!

When Joe was a teenager, his sister Patricia paid the tuition for a correspondence course in cartooning, the only formal art training he received. Joe says, "My cartooning is a family affair: Mom started it, Dad posed for it, and Trish paid for it! My other brothers and sister provided the inspiration!"

As pastor of Kenner, Louisiana's First Baptist Church (metro New Orleans), Joe is well-known as a storyteller, a writer of magazine articles, and cartoons. His weekly article is available free over the internet by sending your address to his church at "fbck1@compuserve.com." Baptist Press runs one of Joe's cartoons daily on its website: bp.news/lighterside. Other newspapers such as the Charlotte Observer, the Northeast Journal (Tupelo, MS), and the Mountain Eagle (Jasper, AL) run his cartoon on their weekly religion page. A dozen or so weekly Baptist state papers run his cartoon on their editorial page.

Contact Joe at his church website, www.fbckenner.org, or at:

P.O. Box 1357
Kenner, LA 70063
Phone (504) 466-5381

Order Form

Laughter's Chief Counsel
Luther Beauchamp
P.O. Box 10, Chiefland, FL 32644
Toll-free 1-888-568-6677

<u>Description</u>	<u>Quantity</u>	<u>Total Price</u>
Books: $10.00		
I'll Try to Be Short. . .	_____	_____
Legal Shorts, Not Briefs	_____	_____
Video Tapes: $20.00		
LIVE! At the Opryland Hotel	_____	_____
Audio Tapes: $10.00		
Love is a Laughing Matter	_____	_____
Secretaries are Not Secondary	_____	_____
Amnesia, Ambrosia & Amnesty	_____	_____
LIVE! At the Opryland Hotel	_____	_____
Set of three (3) audio tapes		
$20.00 per set	_____	_____
1 Book and two (2) audio tapes		
$20.00 per set	_____	_____
"Short Stack"		
1 Book and three (3) audio tapes	_____	_____
$25.00 per stack		
"Not-So-Short Stack"	_____	_____
Video, 1 book, and three (3) audio tapes		

Subtotal	$	_____
Please add Shipping & Handling	$	3.95
TOTAL	$	_____

Name _____

Address _____

City, State, Zip _____

❏ Mastercard   ❏ VISA   ❏ Check/Money Order

Credit Card Number _____

Exp. Date _____

Signature _____